Oxford International Resources

1

Skills

Writing and Grammar

Claire Sharkey

OXFORD

Great Clarendon Street, Oxford, OX2 6DP, United Kingdom

Oxford University Press is a department of the University of Oxford. It furthers the University's objective of excellence in research, scholarship, and education by publishing worldwide. Oxford is a registered trade mark of Oxford University Press in the UK and in certain other countries.

© Oxford University Press 2024

The moral rights of the authors have been asserted

First published in 2024

All rights reserved. No part of this publication may be reproduced, stored in a retrieval system, or transmitted, in any form or by any means, without the prior permission in writing of Oxford University Press, or as expressly permitted by law, by licence or under terms agreed with the appropriate reprographics rights organization. Enquiries concerning reproduction outside the scope of the above should be sent to the Rights Department, Oxford University Press, at the address above.

You must not circulate this work in any other form and you must impose this same condition on any acquirer

British Library Cataloguing in Publication Data
Data available

9781382046060

10 9 8 7 6 5 4 3 2 1

Paper used in the production of this book is a natural, recyclable product made from wood grown in sustainable forests.

The manufacturing process conforms to the environmental regulations of the country of origin.

Printed in China by Golden Cup

Acknowledgements
The publisher and authors would like to thank the following for permission to use photographs and other copyright material:

Cover: Andrea Manzati

Photos: p12 (t): oldbunyip/Shutterstock; p12 (mr): Joe Gough/Shutterstock; p12 (bm): Tatiana Popova/Shutterstock; p12 (ml): KULISH VIKTORIIA/Shutterstock; p12 (br): Photodisc/Getty; p12 (bl): M. Unal Ozmen/Shutterstock; p30 (t): IconLauk/Shutterstock; p30 (b): IconLauk/Shutterstock; p32 (a): Alexander Baluev/Shutterstock; p32 (b): Sakarin Sawasdinaka/Shutterstock; p32 (c): Mega Pixel/Shutterstock; p32 (d): 5PH/Shutterstock; p32 (e): Y Photo Studio/Shutterstock; p32 (f): Hemera Technologies Inc.; p34 (l): Colorfuel Studio/Shutterstock; p34 (r): Victor Brave/Shutterstock; p35: Colorfuel Studio/Shutterstock; p36 (a): KanKhem/Shutterstock; p36 (b): Yefym Turkin/Shutterstock; p36 (c): mything/Shutterstock; p36 (d): yusufdemirci/Shutterstock; p36 (e): Colorfuel Studio/Shutterstock; p38: agefotostock /Alamy Stock Photo; p40: Hakase_420/Shutterstock; p42 (br): Nigel Kitching/Sylvie Poggio; p44 (a): Photodisc/Getty; p44 (b): M. Unal Ozmen/Shutterstock; p44 (c): Picsfive/Shutterstock; p46: BlueRingMedia/Shutterstock; p47: BlueRingMedia/Shutterstock; p52: Dollar Bill Studios/Shutterstock; p64: BeataGFX/Shutterstock; p66: Svetlana_Smirnova/Shutterstock; p68 (tl): Chursina Viktoriia/Shutterstock; p68 (tm): Shutterstock; p68 (tr): Africa Studio/Shutterstock; p68 (bl): Siam Pukkato/123RF.com; p68 (br): successo images/Shutterstock; p70: WhiteJack/Shutterstock; p74: yusufdemirci/Shutterstock;

Artwork by Andrea Manzati, Q2A Media and Oxford University Press.

Every effort has been made to contact copyright holders of material reproduced in this book. Any omissions will be rectified in subsequent printings if notice is given to the publisher.

Contents

1 Labels and instructions
Label my classroom	4
Describe a picture	6
Describe animals	8
Use capital letters and full stops	10
Write a list	12
Write instructions	14

2 Stories
Write about myself	16
Write about a story	18
Create a new hero	20
Describe a setting	22
Plan a story	24
Tell a story	26

3 Planning and reports
Describe what I see	28
Describe myself	30
Describe what I like	32
Describe my day	34
Plan my perfect day	36
Write an adventure diary	38

4 Poems and games
Write a poem	40
Make rhymes	42
Write about objects	44
Write an animal poem	46
Describe objects	48
Create a colour poem	50

5 Friends and family
Make plurals	52
Write about the past	54
Write about things we do	56
Describe a friend	58
Describe my hero	60
Write about my family	62

6 Writing to persuade
Spell words for a poster	64
Write about a trip	66
Persuade my teacher	68
Make an advert	70
Write a review	72
Review my year	74

Grammar glossary	76
Grammar practice	78
Little Red Riding Hood	79

1) Labels and instructions

1 Alphabet Writing Race!

Write the letters along the track in lower-case and capital letters.

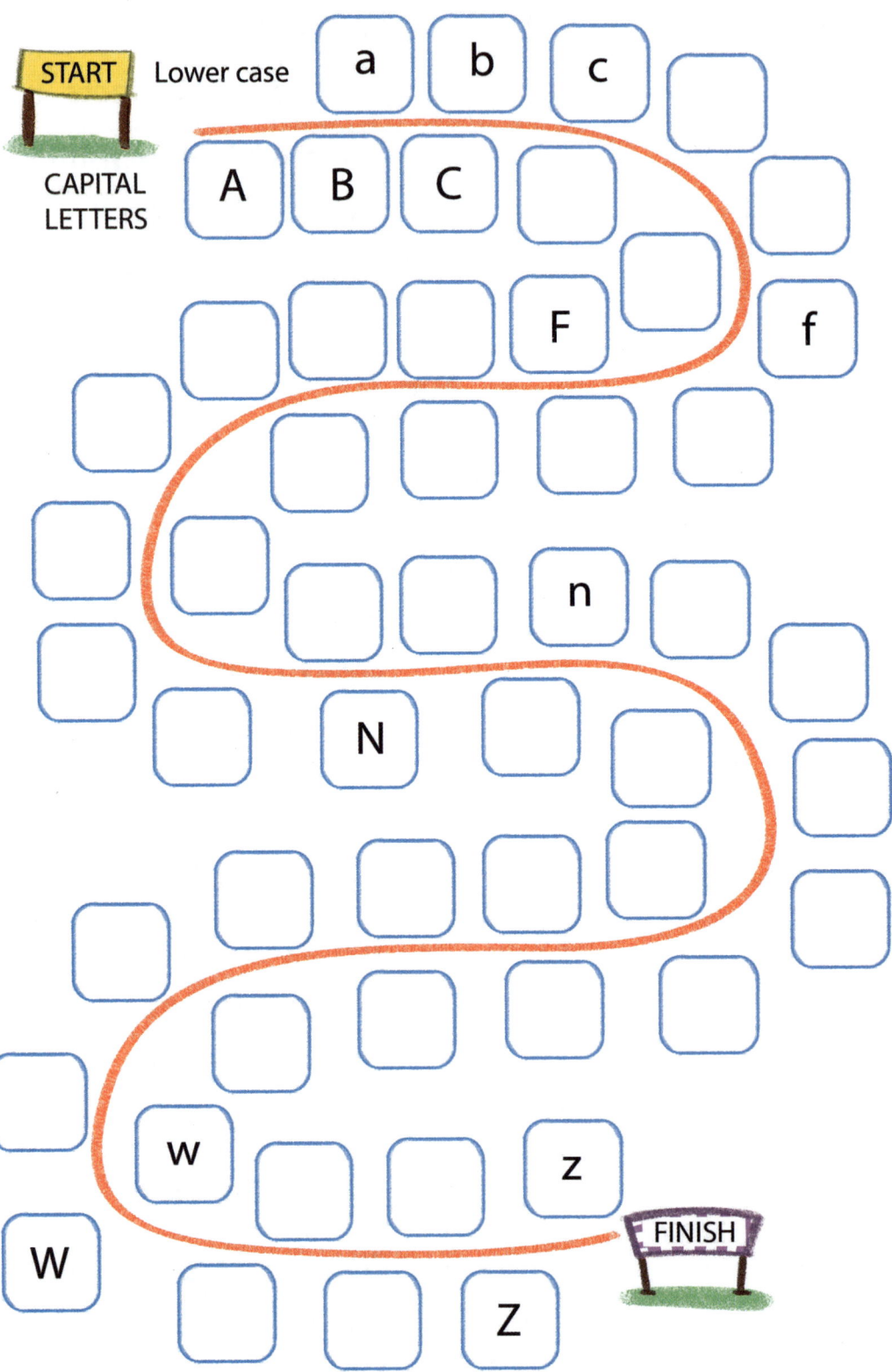

Label my classroom and form letters

2 Make three-letter words using these letters. Write each word in lower-case and then in capital letters.

s a t p i n

tap   TAP

3 Draw a simple picture of your classroom. Label your picture. *10 mins*

books

window

chair

table

pencil

4 Finish these sentences about your picture.

There is a table.

There is a _____

There is a _____

1 Labels and instructions

1 Look at the picture.

What can you see? What is happening?

2 Label the picture using these words.

the bridge   the eggs   the tree   the pond   the fish   the bird

the bridge

Describe a picture and use finger spaces between words

3 Write the sentences correctly using finger spaces.

Ilikebirds.

I like birds.

Ilikeeggs.

Iliketrees.

4 Complete the sentences using the picture.

There is a bridge.

There is a

The bird is

Write your own sentences about the picture. Remember to use finger spaces.

1 Labels and instructions

1 What is a **noun**?

What is an **adjective**?

2 Label the picture using these nouns.

~~grass~~   man   tree   flower   mouse   elephant

Describe animals using adjectives

3 Describe the elephant and the mouse. Use adjectives from the box or your own.

~~strong~~   tall   purple   quiet   big   tiny

strong

4 Describe each animal using the adjectives. Use finger spaces between words.

The elephant is strong and

1 Labels and instructions

💬 **1** Look closely at this picture. What can you see?

2 Label the picture using these words.   ball   ~~rope~~   girl   tree   slide   wall

3 Complete these sentences. Add the right capital letter and a full stop.

T̲ he girl is running .̲

[T   S   E]

____veryone looks happy____

____he boy is skipping____

____lides are fun____

10

Write using capital letters and full stops

4. You are playing in the park. Write sentences to say what you do. Use capital letters and full stops.

I climb the wall.

1 Labels and instructions

💬 **1** Look at the picture.

What is this?

What do you need to make a sandwich?

What is your favourite sandwich?

2 Label these pictures using the words in the box.

| bread | banana | ~~peanut butter~~ | knife | plate |

peanut butter

Write a list

3 Draw everything you need to make your favourite sandwich.

My favourite sandwich

10 mins

4 Write a list of things you need.

You will need:

1 Labels and instructions

 1 Play 'Follow the leader' with a partner. Use these instructions.

- Pat your stomach.
- Stand up.
- Rub hands together.
- Turn around.
- Put hands on heads.
- Sit down.

2 What is missing from the instructions in the box?

Add capital letters and full stops.

Follow the leader

Put your hands on your heads .

___ub your hands together___

___at your stomach___

___tand up___

___urn around___

___it down___

Write instructions

3 Complete the instructions for Monkey.

 a  b  c  d

Go   hat   Jump   Put   ~~shoes~~

a Put on your shoes .

b _____ on your _____ .

c _____ for a walk.

d _____ in a puddle!

4 What can Monkey do at the park? Write instructions for him.

bike    Ride your _____

slide    _____

ball    _____

2 Stories

1 A **noun** is a naming word.

What nouns can you see in the picture?

2 Hana and Ayesha are people's names. Names of people start with a capital letter.

Write your name with a capital letter.

Other nouns in the picture are football, food, birds and bicycle. These are not names of people. They begin with a lower-case letter.

Circle the nouns in the box which need a capital letter.

hassan   boy   hana   park   maria   trees   banana   shoes

Write about myself and use capital letters

3 Draw a picture of you and a friend playing at the park. Write labels for the nouns. Use capital letters for names.

10 mins

4 Finish the sentences.

My friend's name is _____

My teacher's name is _____

My school is called _____

Write your own sentence using a name.

_____

_____

2 Stories

1 Guess Who!

Describe one character to a partner, but do not use their name. Can your partner guess who it is?

> They have white hair.

Little Red Riding Hood

Kind Grandma

Big, Bad Wolf

2 Fill in the gaps with **a** or **an**.

Remember, if a word begins with **a**, **e**, **i**, **o** or **u**, we use **an** before it: **an** apple, **an** egg.

Little Red Riding Hood is wearing __a__ cloak with __a__ hood.

a She is carrying _____ basket. In the basket is food for Grandma.

b She goes into the woods. She hears _____ owl.

c Then, _____ wolf steps out from behind _____ tree.

Write about a story using 'a' or 'an'

3 What do you think Little Red Riding Hood has in her basket?

Draw the basket and what she has in it. Add labels.

4 Write two sentences about what is inside the basket. Remember to use **a**, **an** and **the** in your sentences.

2 Stories

1 Little Red Riding Hood is in trouble! Draw a hero who can save her.

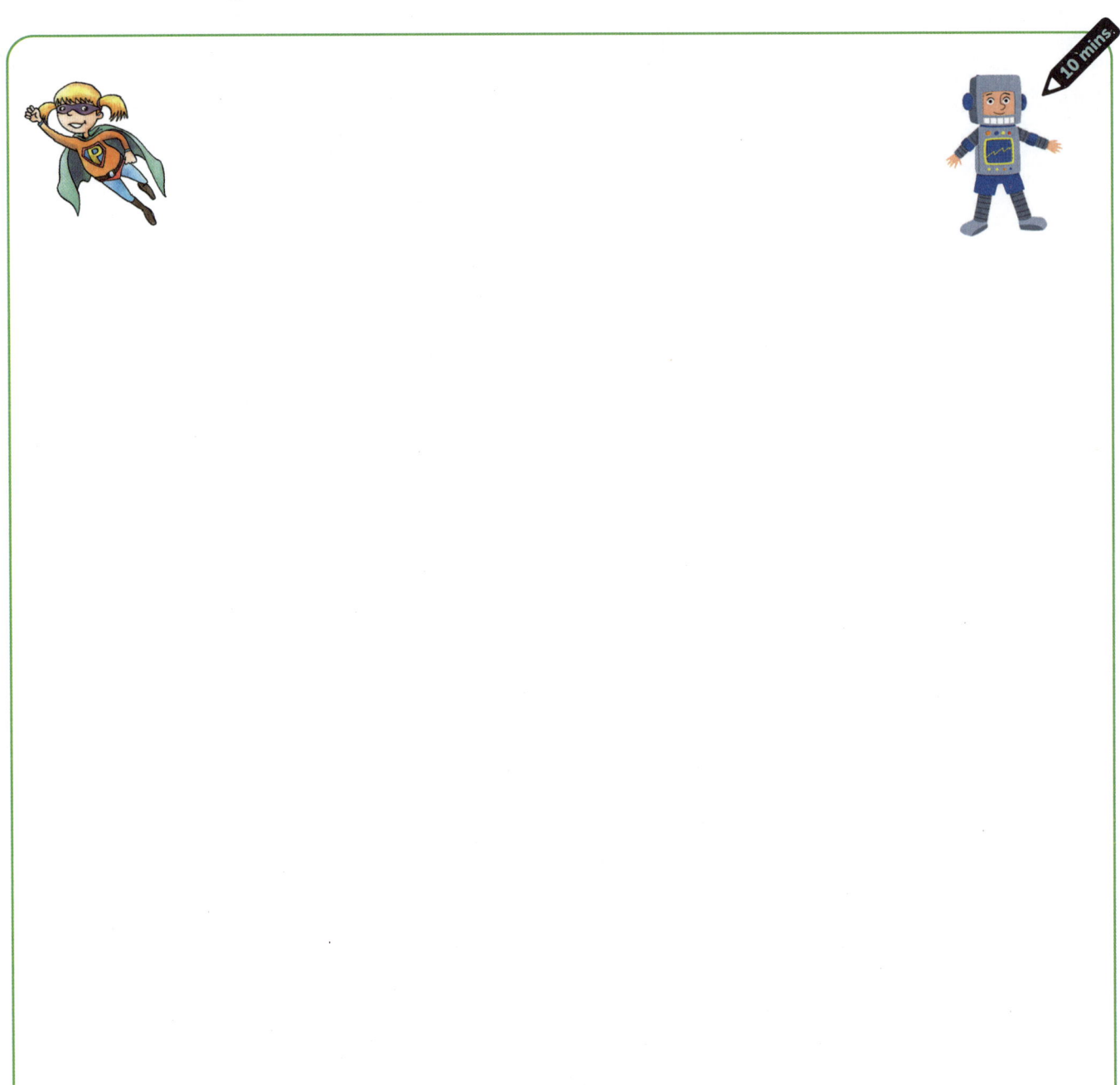

2 Add **adjectives** to describe your hero. Write them around your drawing. You can use the ones in this box or think of your own.

| brave | strong | fast | clever | kind |

Create a new hero

3 Write about your hero.

What does your hero look like?

My new hero is called _____

My hero has _____ hair.

My hero has _____ eyes.

How does your hero act? Include adjectives to describe what they do.

My hero is _____

_____

_____

4 Talk to a partner. Retell the ending of Little Red Riding Hood with your new hero.

Your new hero

2 Stories

1 Imagine you are Little Red Riding Hood in the picture.

What can you see? 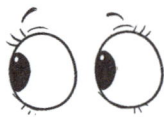   What can you smell?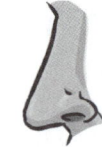

What can you hear?    What can you feel?

2 Label the picture using **nouns**.

| tree | ~~branches~~ | wolf | grass | bird |

Describe a setting

3 Choose the best two **adjectives** to label the pictures with. You can use these or think of your own.

dark   quiet   spooky   cold   yellow
rustling   soft   ~~tall~~   quick

tall

_____   _____   _____
_____   _____   _____

4 Use the adjectives you chose to write a sentence describing each picture.

 The dark branches are tall.

 _____

 _____

23

2 Stories

1 Draw a picture of Little Red Riding Hood's house in the forest.

2 Complete the sentences from the beginning of the story. Use the phrases in the box.

> Grandma's house Once upon a time
> Little Red Riding Hood the big, bad wolf

a _____ a little girl lived in

a dark forest with her mum.

b She wore a red coat and her name was _____

_____ .

c One day, her mum said, "Please take this basket to _____

_____ ."

d On her way, Little Red Riding Hood met _____

_____ .

Plan a story

3 Choose the best **adjective** in each sentence.

   a The wolf talked to Little Red Riding Hood but she knew he was _____ (good/bad).

   b Little Red Riding Hood felt _____ (scared/excited) so she ran away very quickly.

   c It was a _____ (short/long) way to Grandma's house and she was tired when she got to the door.

   d A voice said "Come in, Little Red Riding Hood." Little Red Riding Hood felt _____ (afraid/happy), that did not sound like Grandma…

4 Plan the end of the story. Make notes about how your hero saves Little Red Riding Hood from the wolf.

> All the better for… gobbling you up!

Draw your hero

Little Red Riding Hood saw it was not Grandma.

It was the wolf! Then

2 Stories

1. Write the story of Little Red Riding Hood. Use your answers and plan from the last lesson. The pictures will help you.

Once upon a time

Tell a story

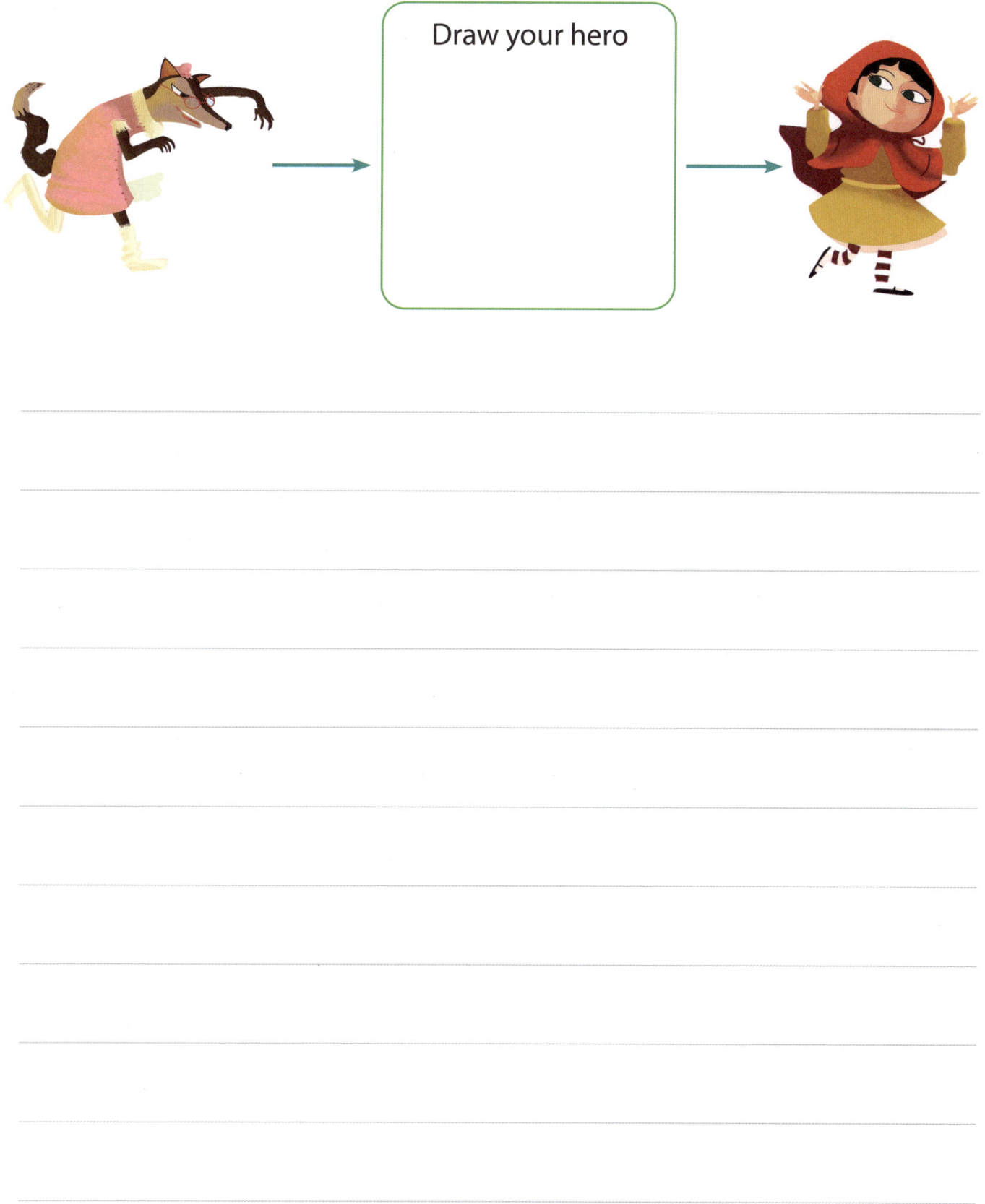

2 Reread your writing to check that it makes sense.
Share your story with a partner.

3 Planning and reports

💬 **1** What do you see in this picture?

2 Circle the capital letter and full stop in each sentence.

(T)he train is green(.)

a The sky is blue.

b There are lots of trees.

c There are small dinosaurs and big dinosaurs.

d The dinosaurs are different colours.

Describe what I see using capital letters and full stops

3 Write these sentences. Put the words in the correct order.

grass   The   green.   is

The grass is green.

a   smiled.   The   dinosaur

_____

b   moved   train   slowly.   The

_____

c   dinosaur   feet.   The   stomped   his

_____

4 Imagine you are one of the people in the picture. Write about what you can see.

_____

_____

_____

Read your sentences to a partner. Ask them to draw a little 😊 next to their favourite sentence.

3 Planning and reports

1 In each speech bubble, write a question you could ask your partner.

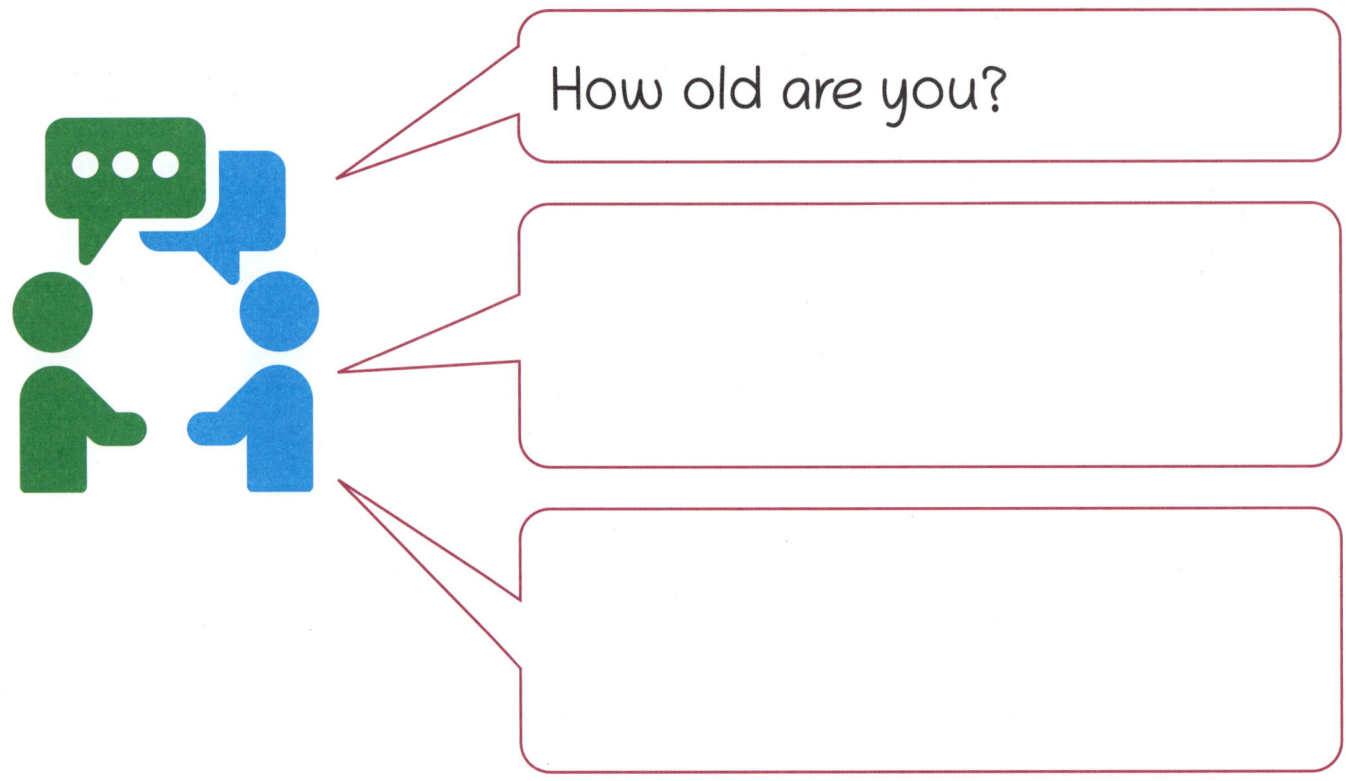

How old are you?

2 Write your partner's answers in the speech bubbles.

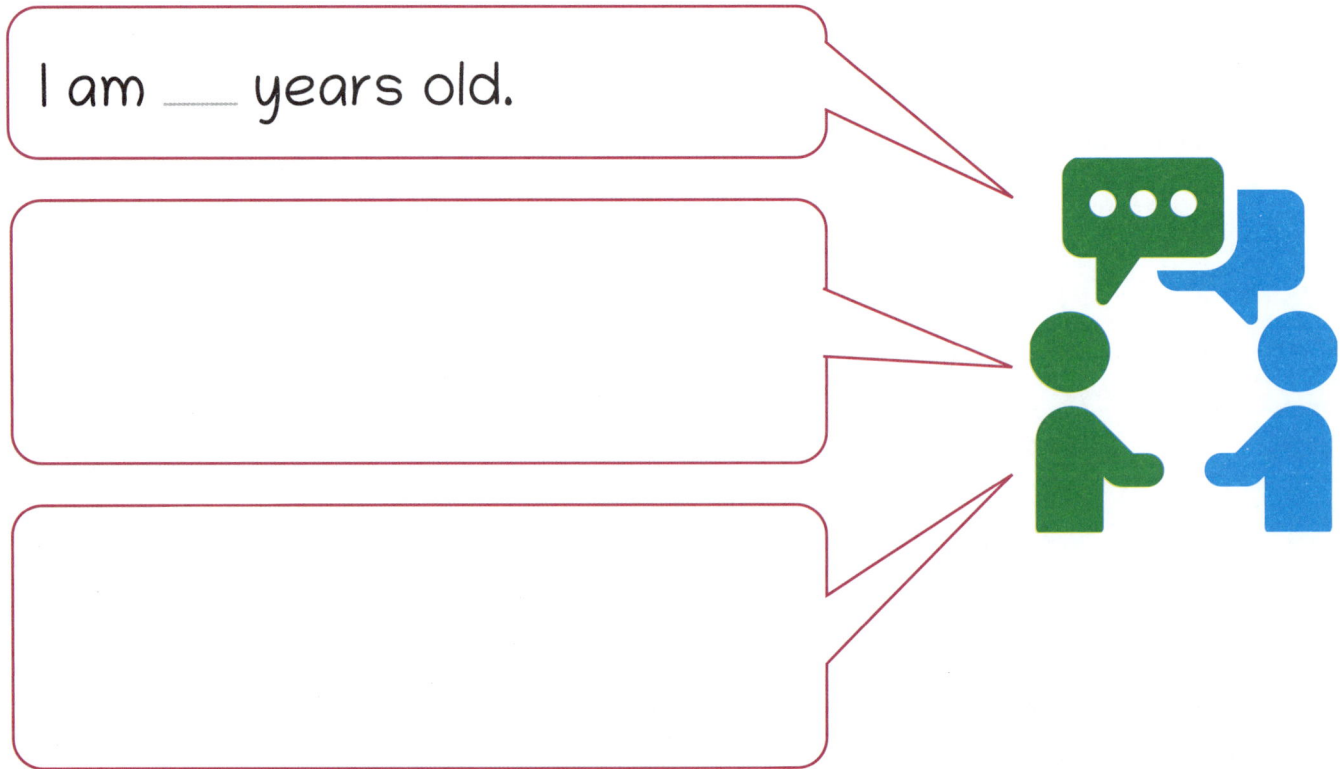

I am ___ years old.

Describe myself using I

3 Spot the mistakes!

Ⓒircle the things that are wrong. Then write the sentences correctly.

⒤ am 5 years old◯

I am 5 years old.

i have two sisterz.

I like to plai football

4 Write three sentences about yourself. Each sentence should start with **I**.

I am called

I like

3 Planning and reports

💬 **1** What foods do you like? What foods do you not like?

2 Draw lines to match each food to its picture.
Then write an adjective to describe each food.

pizza

curry

nuts

fruit —— sweet

wrap

32

Describe what I like

3 What is your favourite food? Draw it here and add labels.

10 mins

4 Complete the sentences about food.

I like _____

_____

I don't like _____

_____

If I could only eat one food, I would eat _____

_____

because _____

_____

3 Planning and reports

1 What have you done today?

"I cleaned my teeth."
"I walked to school."
"I ate my breakfast."

2 Draw a picture of what you did. Then write a sentence.

I woke up.

Describe my day

3 What will you do after school?

I will go to the park.

My dad will pick me up.

After that, I will play with my sister.

_____

_____

_____

4 How did you feel today? Write in the thought bubble.

I had fun at school.

I felt tired.

I enjoyed my breakfast.

35

3 Planning and reports

 1 Read Omar's diary.

> Thursday 22nd May
>
> Dear diary,
>
> Today I woke up and had some  for breakfast. Then, I went to  and played with my . After that, I went to a big . It was at Hana's house. It was so much fun. I went home feeling .

2 Add these time words to Omar's diary.

> Then   Finally   After that

Today I woke up and had some eggs for breakfast.

_____ I went to school and played with my friends.

_____, I went to a party.

It was Hana's birthday. It was so much fun.

_____, I went home feeling tired.

Plan my perfect day

3 What would be your perfect day? Draw and write what would happen.

First,

Then,

After that,

Finally,

3 Planning and reports

1 Imagine that yesterday you woke up here! What did you see?

2 There was lots to do in this world! What did you do first? Circle three activities.

- I ran in the forest
- I flew over the city
- I bounced on the cloud
- I jumped in the water

3 Write **adjectives** to describe how you would feel.

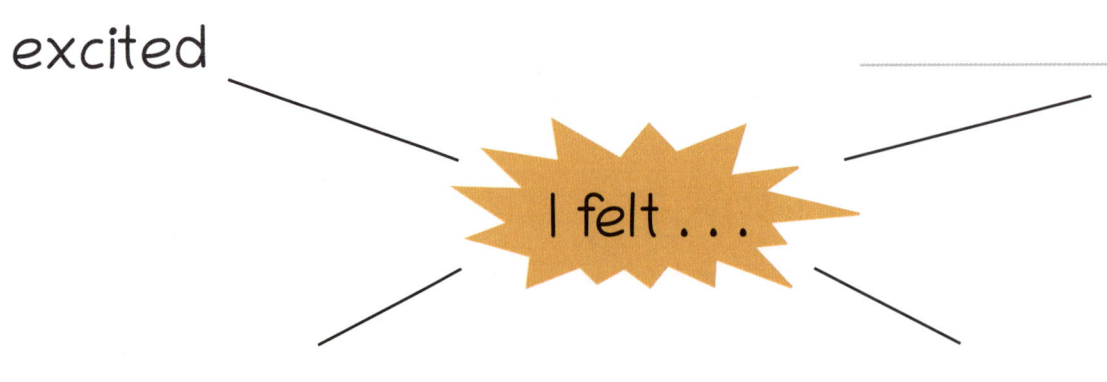

excited

I felt . . .

Write an adventure diary and use adjectives

4 Use these ideas to write a diary entry about your exciting adventure.

Date

Dear diary,

Yesterday was fun. First,

4 Poems and games

1 Read this poem.

Can you find the words that rhyme? Circle them!

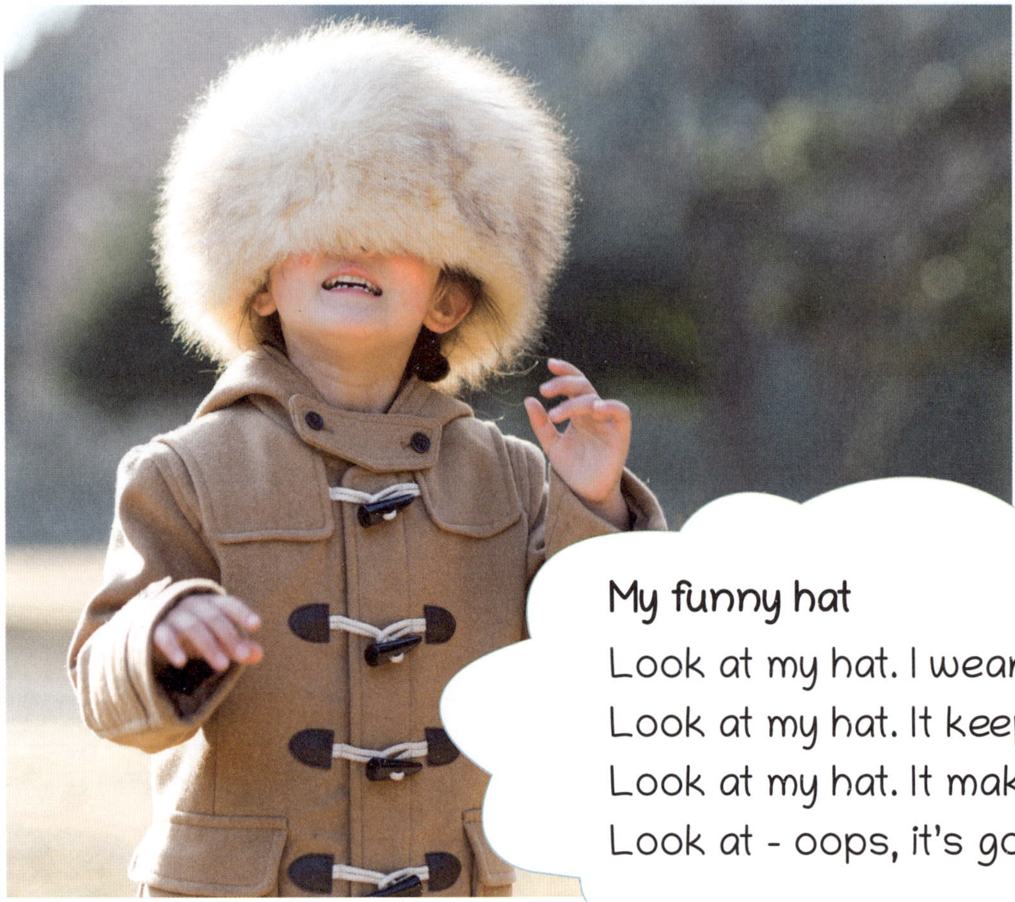

My funny hat

Look at my hat. I wear it for fun.
Look at my hat. It keeps off the sun.
Look at my hat. It makes me seem tall.
Look at - oops, it's going to fall!

2 Draw lines to match the rhyming words.

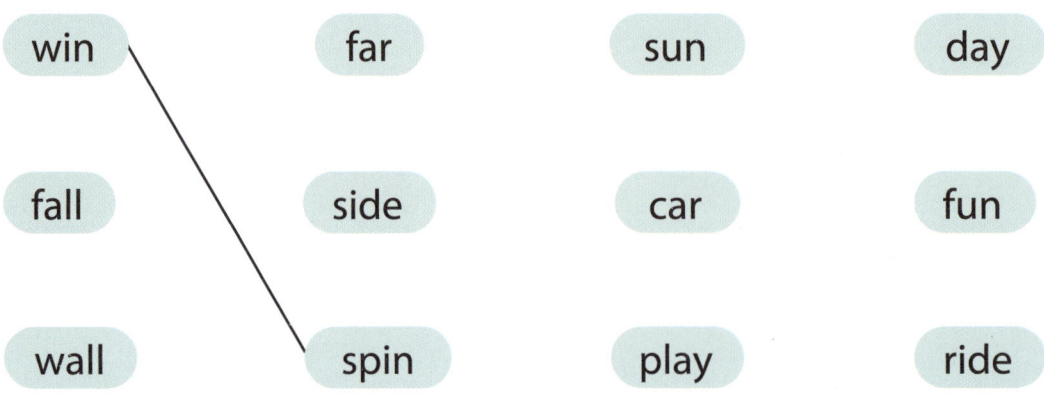

Write a poem

3 Choose one of the toys from the list. Draw a picture of you playing with the toy and add labels.

| bat |
| car |
| ball |
| bike |
| teddy |
| blocks |
| train |
| doll |
| robot |

4 Write a poem about a toy. You can continue this poem about a ball or write about another toy.

| tall | call | crawl | hall |

See my ball. Look at it fall.

See my ball. Up on the wall.

4 Poems and games

1 Look carefully at this picture. Can you spot the three things that rhyme with **chat?** Circle them!

2 Say each word aloud. Then write it under the word it rhymes with.

~~day~~   bad   be   fun   run   had   me   say

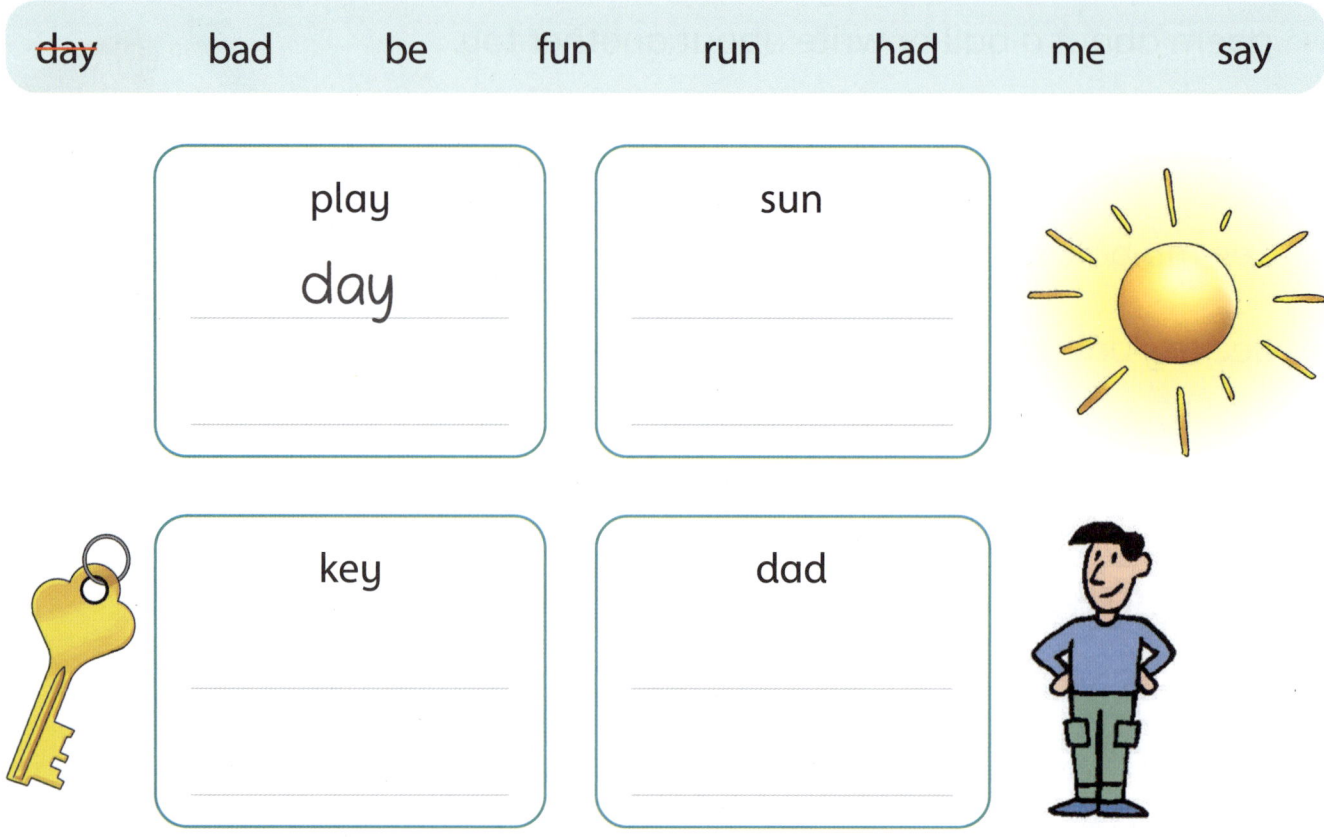

play

day

sun

key

dad

Make rhymes

3 Complete this poem, using the words below.

> fun   play   be

I had been indoors all **day,**

And I wanted to go out and _____.

It was hot in the garden, in the **sun,**

But I was still having so much _____.

Under a pot, I found a **key,**

How exciting! What could it _____?

4 Write your own poem. You can use rhyming words from **2** to help.

4 Poems and games

1. What am I?

   Pick a picture. Describe it to a partner, but don't say what it is.

2. Draw lines to match the sentences to the pictures.

   I buzz.

   I go on roads.

   I am very hot.

   You can eat me.

   I fly up to space.

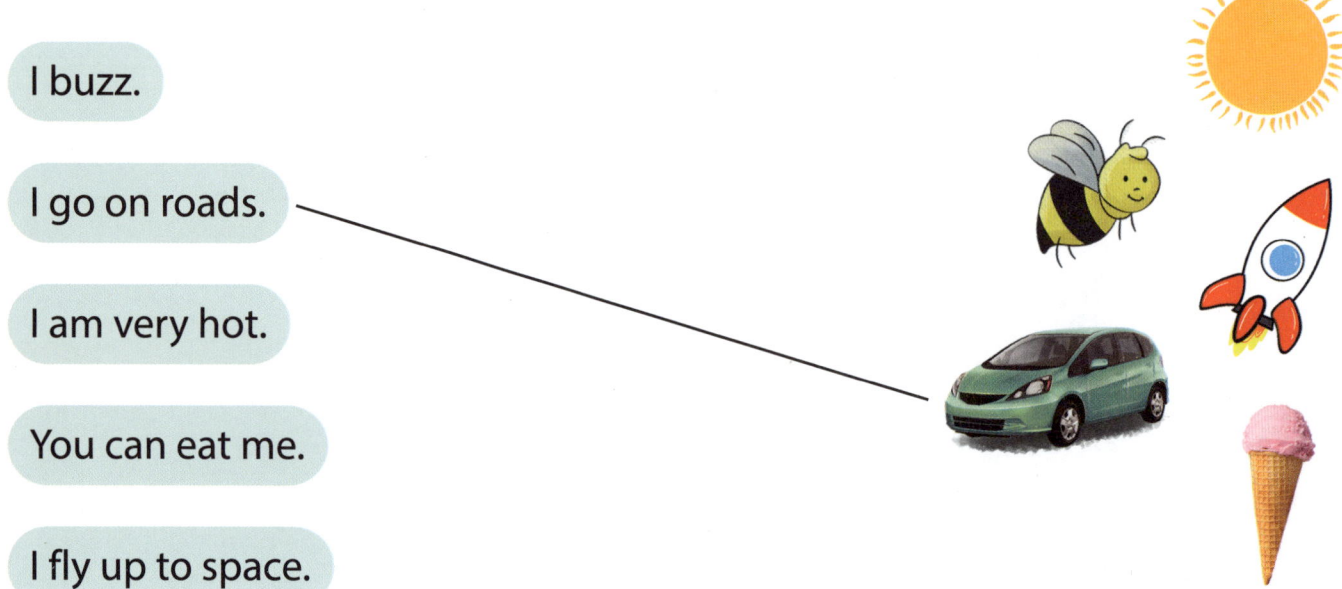

Write about objects using adjectives

3 Choose another picture from **1**. Describe it. The words in the box could help.

> cold   animal   yellow   fast   wheels   food   tasty   legs   high   ride

I have _____

I am _____

You can _____

4 Choose an object in the classroom. Don't tell anyone what it is! Write two sentences to describe it.

It is sharp. I use it to write.

_____

_____

_____

_____

_____

Swap books with a partner. Can you guess what their object is?

4 Poems and games

1 Pick an animal. Describe it to a partner. Can your partner guess which animal you are describing?

It lives in the sea.

It eats grass.

tiger · lion · turtle · bear · monkey · giraffe

2 Write each animal's name under the right **adjectives**.

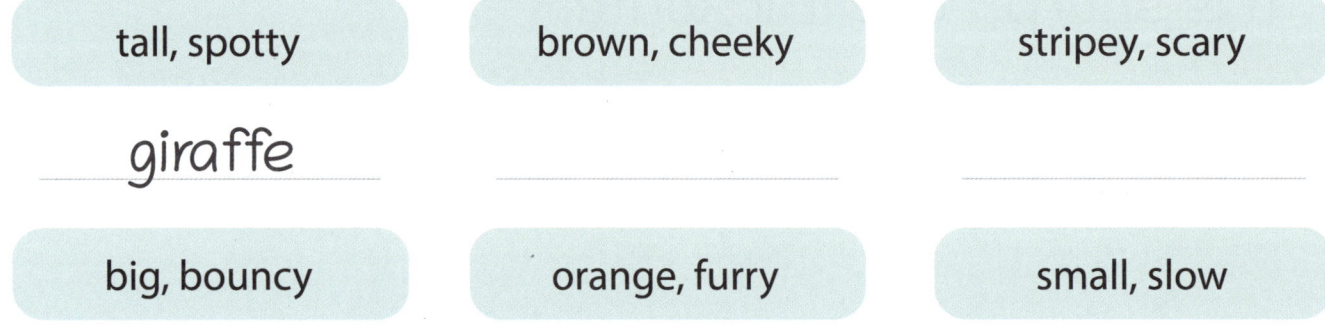

tall, spotty	brown, cheeky	stripey, scary
giraffe		

big, bouncy	orange, furry	small, slow

3 What is your favourite animal?

Draw a picture of the animal. Add labels to describe it.

Write a poem describing an animal

4 Write a poem about your favourite animal.

Big, bouncy bear,
Always eats honey.
Lives in the forest,
Likes to be funny!

What does it look like?

What does it eat?

Where does it live?

What does it like to do?

4 Poems and games

1 Look at these pictures with a partner. How would you describe these things?

2 Draw lines to match two **adjectives** to each picture.

yellow

hot

hard

cosy

shiny

soft

bright

red

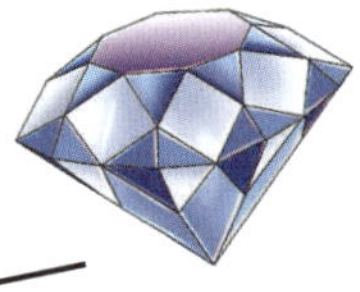

Describe objects

3 Finish these sentences.

As shiny as a diamond.

As _____ as a pillow.

As _____ as a fire.

As _____ as a star.

4 Write sentences to describe things in your classroom.

As full as the waste bin.

As _____ as a _____.

_____

_____

_____

4 Poems and games

1. Pick a colour! What do you think of when you see this colour? How does it make you feel?

orange   red   blue   yellow   purple   green

2. What is your favourite colour? Write it in the box in the centre.

Then write things this colour reminds you of in the other boxes.

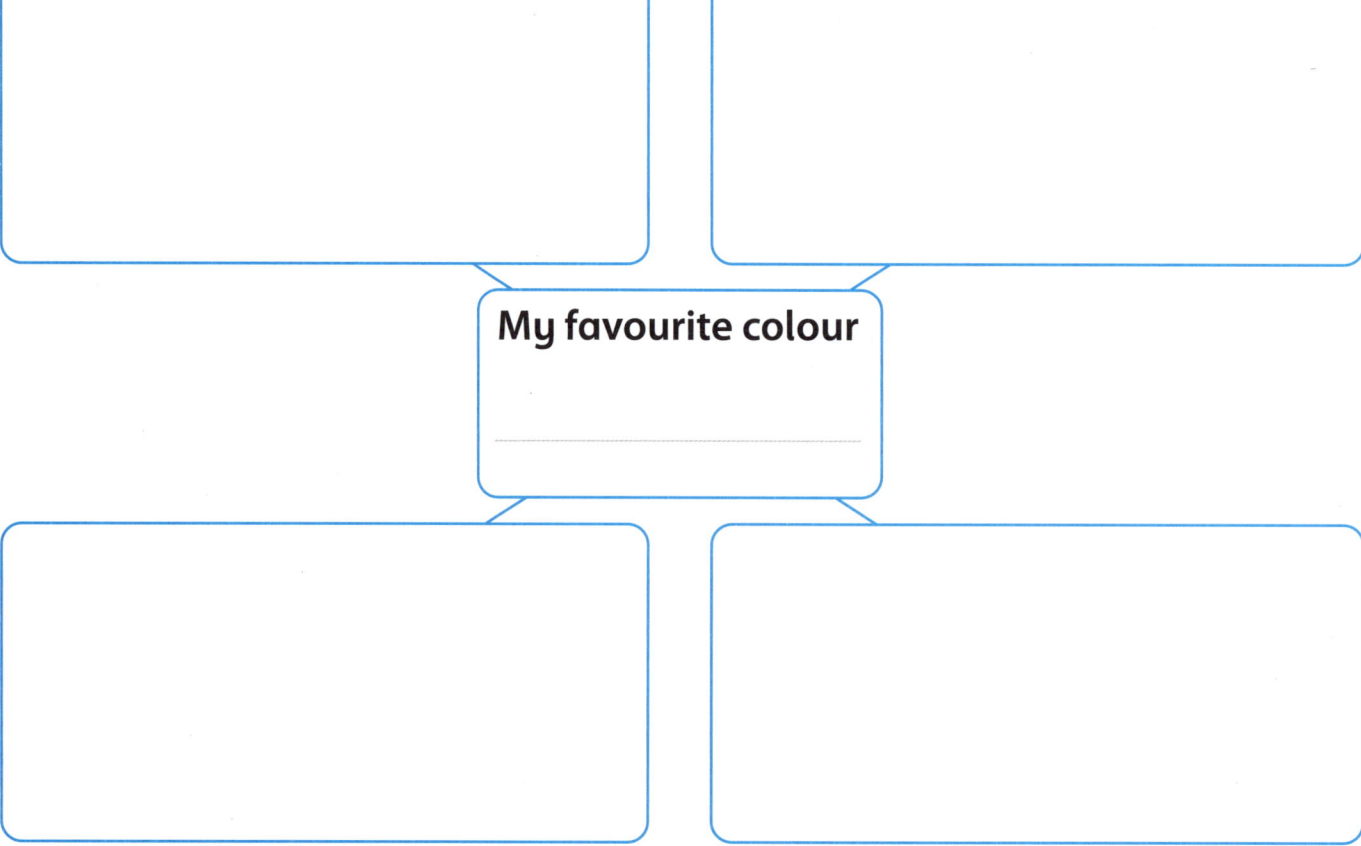

Create a poem describing a colour

3 Write a poem about colours. Use your notes from **2**.

Yellow is the sun shining in the sky.

_____ is _____

4 Read your poem to yourself. Then share it with a partner.

5 Friends and family

1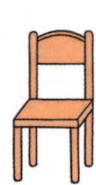

Write examples for each type of **noun**.

Use the pictures to help you.

person	place	thing

What does the word **plural** mean? Clue:

2 Change these nouns to the plural.

 One **boy**    Lots of boys

 One **door**    Lots of _____

 One **desk**    Lots of _____

 One **book**    _____

Make plurals using '-s' or '-es'

3 If a word ends with one of these sounds, we add **-es** to change it to the plural: sh, ch, ss, s, x, z.

Change these words into the plural.

box = boxes

dish =

glass =

bus =

4 Mum is sorting out the cupboards. Write a list of what she finds.

There are two mugs.

What are you doing in there?

5 Friends and family

1 What is a **verb**?

Match the verbs to the pictures.

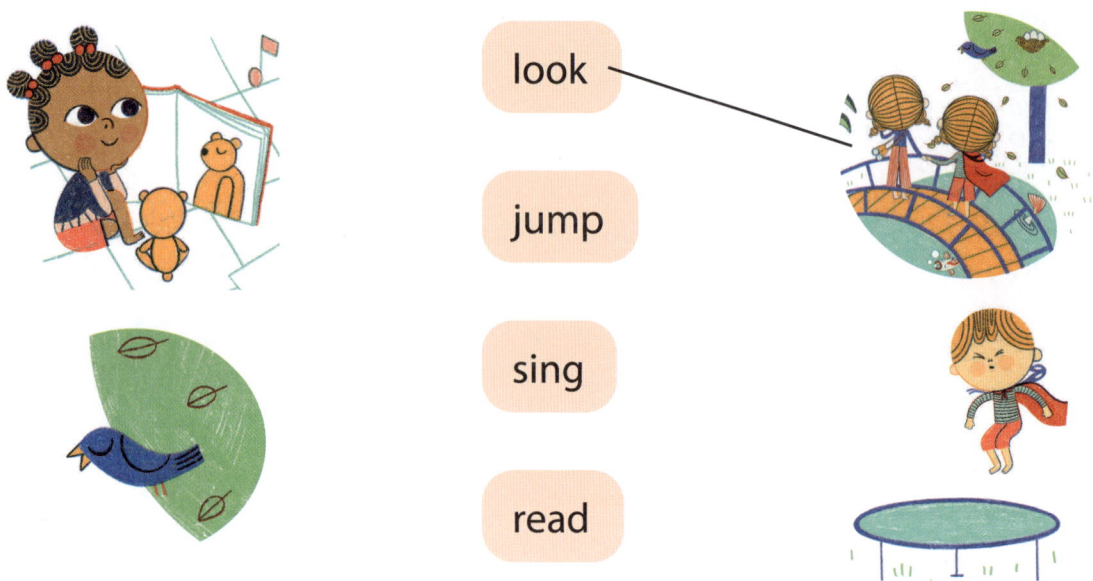

2 Verb hunt! How many verbs can you think of?

Verb hunt!

Take turns to choose one of your verbs. Act out the word and see if your partner can guess it.

Write about the past using '-ed'

3 Change these verbs to the **past tense**. Add **-ed** to each one.

walk = walked finish = _____

play = _____ climb = _____

fold = _____ jump = _____

4 Dad asked you to help tidy the house.

Complete the sentences. Add **-ed** to the verbs.

(help) I helped Dad to clean the house.

(clean) I _____ my bedroom.

(brush) I _____ the floor.

(wash) _____

(fold) _____

Write some more sentences in the past tense.

_____

_____

_____

5 Friends and family

1 What are the children doing in this picture?

2 The ending **-ing** tells us a **verb** is happening now. Add **-ing** to these words.

play = playing

draw =

talk =

laugh =

dream =

Write about things we do using '-ing'

3 Complete the table.

Word	+ing	=
pull	ing	pulling
paint	ing	
look	ing	
think	ing	
	ing	singing
	ing	wishing
	ing	cooking

4 Jesse and her friends are having a lot of fun. Write sentences to describe what they are doing. Use as many verbs ending in **-ing** as you can.

They are having fun.

57

5 Friends and family

1 Look at this picture.
- How are the children feeling?
- What is a friend?
- What makes our friends special?

2 In each star, write what a good friend is or does. A friend . . .

Describe a friend

3 What makes a good friend? Write sentences to describe what makes a good friend. Use your ideas from **2** and these words to help you.

> honest   kind   caring   fun   playful   loving   helpful

A good friend _____

_____

A good friend _____

_____

4 Draw a picture of your friend. Describe a fun time you had together.

5 Friends and family

1 Who is your hero?

Write their name here. _____

Why are they your hero?

My hero is my mum.

He is my hero because he is kind.

2 What does your hero look like?
Draw a picture of your hero.

Describe my hero

3 How does your hero act?

Label your hero with words that describe them. You can choose from these words or write your own.

thoughtful	caring	kind	honest	brave
happy	funny	helpful	clever	strong

4 Describe your hero. Write two or three sentences. Say why you chose them.

I chose my hero because they are very brave and caring.

5 Friends and family

1 Look at this picture of a family. Who is in your family? What do you like to do together?

2 Write a list of the people in your family and what you like to do with them.

Family member	What you like to do
Mum	We bake cookies.

Write about my family

3 Draw lines to complete the sentences.

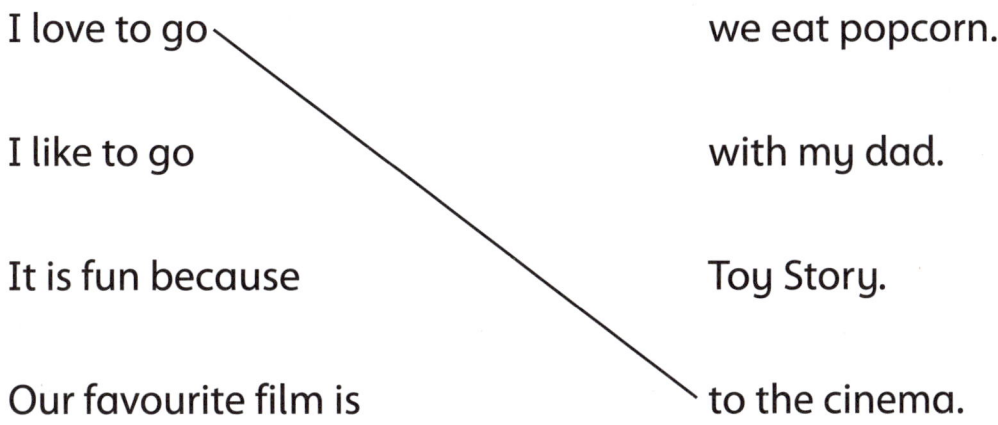

I love to go — to the cinema.

I like to go — with my dad.

It is fun because — we eat popcorn.

Our favourite film is — Toy Story.

4 Choose one of your family members. Write about what you like to do together.

I love to spend time with my _____

Our favourite thing to do is _____

_____

_____

_____

We like it because _____

_____

6 Writing to persuade

1 Read the poster. What is it about?

2 Complete the sentences about the Teddy Bear Picnic. Use these words.

| ~~be~~ | are | friend | Come | Do | me | my |

It will _be_ a great day.

_____ along to the Teddy Bear Picnic.

Bring a _____.

We _____ ready for a picnic.

I will bring _____ favourite teddy.

_____ you want to come along with _____?

Spell tricky words for a poster

3 The writer adds more words to the poster. But they make some mistakes.
- Circle the spelling mistakes.
- Then, write each one correctly on the lines.

(Com) and join us on Saturday in hte park. Bring yur frends. The day will be ful of fun and games. Thre will be sum prizes.

Come
_____
_____
_____
_____
_____

4 Use each word in a sentence for the poster.

`once` This special picnic happens once a year.

`you` _____

`there` _____

`some` _____

6 Writing to persuade

1 Read this advert aloud.

Would you go on this trip? Why?

Come on a journey through this beautiful forest.

Book your ticket now for this wonderful trip.

FOREST TRIP

You never know what you will see.

2 Rewrite these sentences. Add **and** in the right place.

There is so much to see do.

There is so much to see and do.

a We will see flowers trees.

b The flowers are red pink.

Write about a trip, using 'and' to join phrases

3 Join the sentence parts together. Draw lines to connect them using **and**.

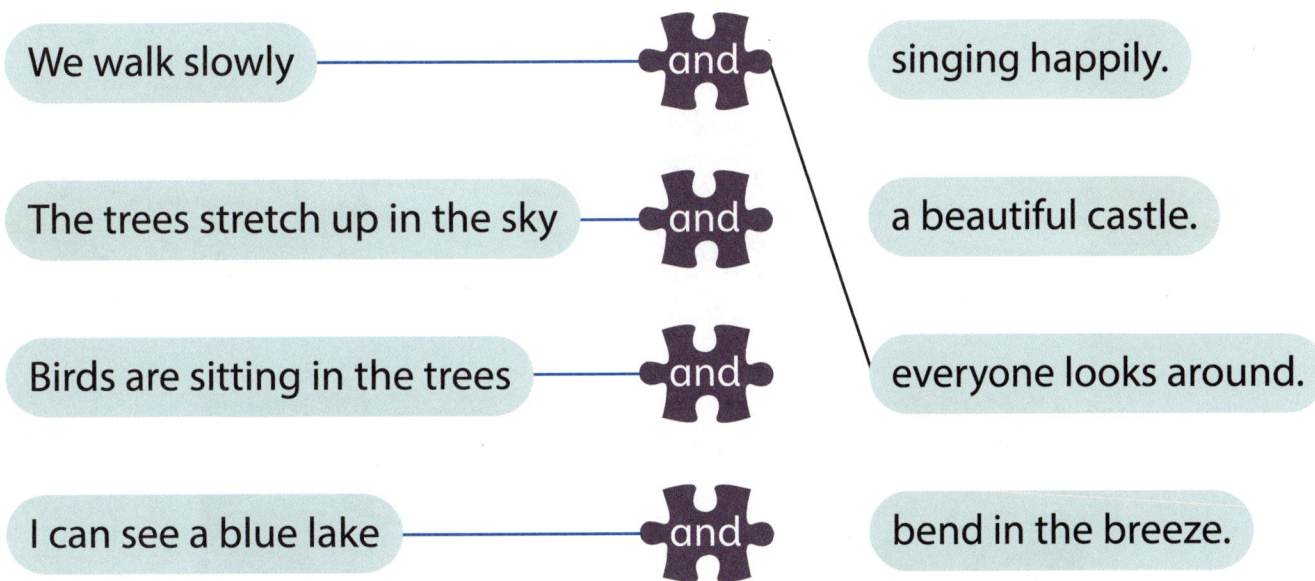

4 Imagine what you will see and do in the forest.

Complete these sentences. Add another sentence of your own using **and**.

In the forest, I can see butterflies and _____

_____

We will explore the hidden castle and _____

_____

_____

_____

_____

6 Writing to persuade

1 What is your favourite dessert? Why do you like it?

2 Draw your favourite dessert here. Add labels to describe it.

Choose words to persuade my teacher

3 What are the best things about your favourite dessert?

Write notes here. You can use these words and add your own.

| creamy | tasty | chocolate | on the top | apple | layers |

My dessert is _____

_____

It has _____

_____

4 Imagine your school decides to make a new dessert.

Persuade your teacher to choose your favourite.

Write two sentences using your notes and these ideas.

| you will love it | it has healthy fruit | it is easy to make | we deserve a treat | children like it |

We should have this dessert because _____

_____

_____

_____

69

6 Writing to persuade

1. Label the features of this advert. Draw lines.

   - food name
   - picture
   - caption

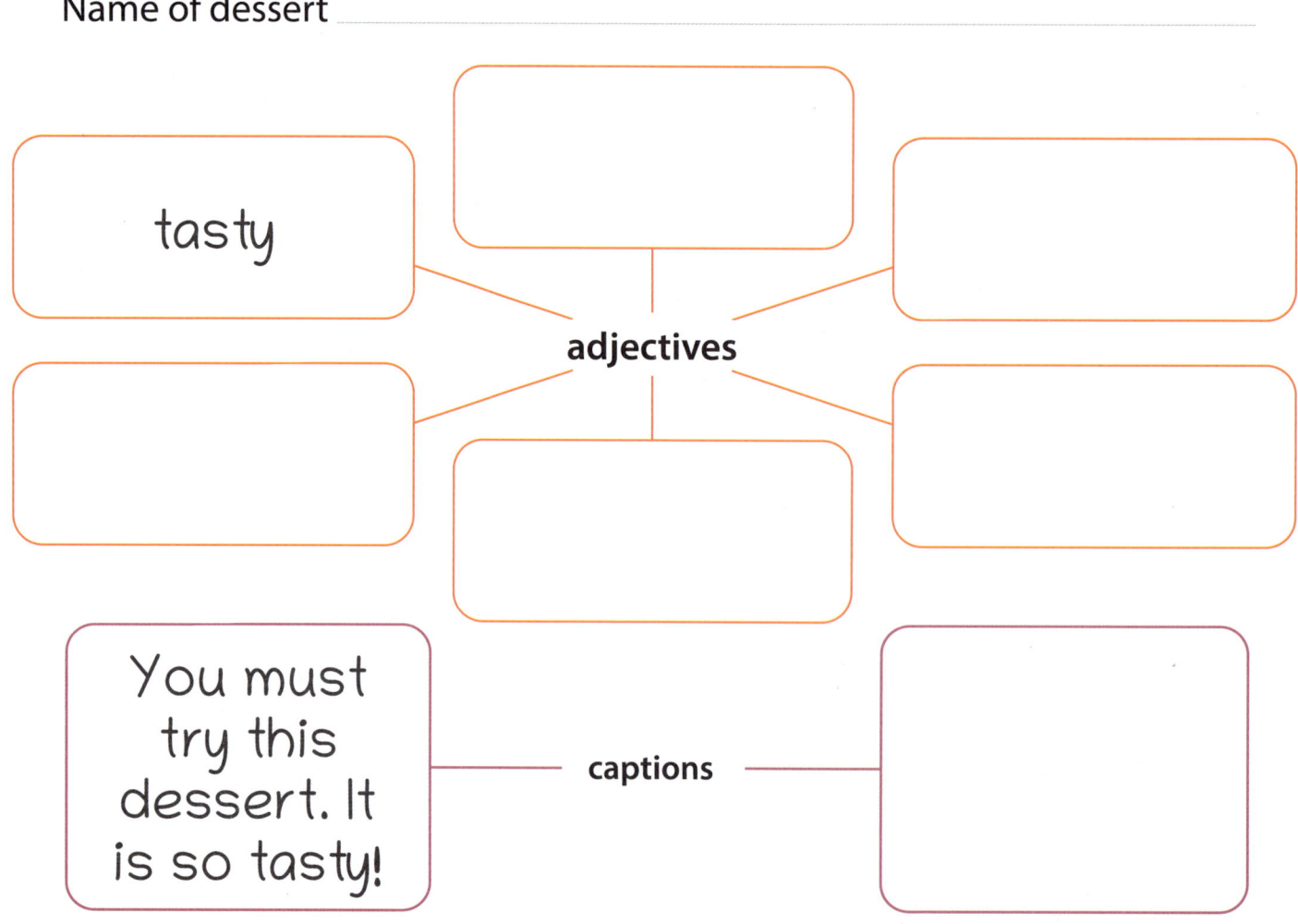

2. Remember your favourite dessert from the last lesson? Today you are going to design a poster for your dessert. Plan your poster here.

   Name of dessert _____

   adjectives
   - tasty
   -
   -
   -
   -

   captions
   - You must try this dessert. It is so tasty!
   -

Make an advert

3 Create your poster. Include:
- the name of the dessert
- a drawing with labels
- some sentences to describe it.

4 Read your writing to a partner. Can you spot any mistakes? Correct them.

6 Writing to persuade

1. Talk about your favourite book or TV show. Make notes about what happens.

2. Draw your favourite character.

My favourite character

3. Label your drawing with **adjectives** to describe the character. Choose from the box or write your own.

funny   happy   brave   kind   tall   small   fast   slow

Write a review

4 Complete the review.

My favourite book or TV show is _____

My favourite character is _____

Because they are _____

What happens? _____

You should read or see this because   it is interesting.   it is exciting.

I would rate it _____ out of 5.

6 Writing to persuade

1 Look at these questions about school.

What do you like learning about?

What do you like about school?

2 It is near the end of our school year. Write notes for each of these questions.

What are you proud of?
What do you like learning about?
What was the best thing about this year?

Use the past tense to review my year

3 Write a review of your year. Use your notes to help you.

My class: _____

I am proud of _____

_____

_____

I like learning about _____

because _____

_____

_____

The best thing about this year was _____

_____

_____

_____

_____

4 Share your review with a partner.

Grammar glossary

adjective a describing word. It tells you more about a noun.
- The cat is **black**.
- The city is **big** and **exciting**.

capital letter special letters used at the beginning of sentences and for names.
- **T**he story was funny.
- **I**t was **H**ana's turn.

caption the words under a picture. They tell you what the picture is about.

-ed can go at the end of a **verb**. When you add '-ed' it means it happened in the past.
- He help**ed** his mum.
- We walk**ed** to school.

full stop a punctuation mark. It goes at the end of a sentence.
- It is cold today**.**

-ing can go at the end of a **verb**. When you add '-ing', it means it is happening now.
- She is jump**ing** high.
- We are paint**ing** a wall.

noun names of people, places, animals and things. Nouns are things you can touch.
- The **cat** is in the **tree**.
- My **house** is in the **city**.

Grammar glossary

past tense tells us that something has already happened. It happened in the past.
- I **played** a game yesterday.
- This morning, the dog **barked** at the cat.

plural means there is more than one.
- One **girl** went to the park. Two **girls** went to the park.

present tense tells us that something is happening now.
- I **am playing** a game.
- The dog **barks** at the cat.

proper noun names a person, place or date that starts with a capital letter.
- **Hana** lives in **Oman**.
- My teacher is **Miss Kumar**.
- It is **Monday** today.

-s or **-es** go at the end of a word when there is more than one; they show the **plural** of a **noun**.
- There are four **foxes** and two **dogs** at the farm.

verb a doing word.
- I **run** to school.
- We **talk** a lot.
- **Look** at me!

Grammar practice

1 Adjectives are describing words. Underline the adjective in each sentence.

I put on my red shorts.
It was a soft pillow.
He found a pretty shell.

2 Circle the capital letters and full stops.

My mum made a cake.
The ducks quacked.
A bird is singing in the tree.

3 Conjunctions are linking words. Circle the conjunctions in the sentences below.

We had cake and played games.
I like melons but not bananas.
My dad made fish and chips.

4 Commas separate items in a list. Add the missing commas.

Cats chase mice birds and rats.
We need paper pens pencils and glue.
The leaves were yellow red orange and brown.
Put the plates spoons and forks away.

5 A plural means there is more than one. Add 's' to make each word into a plural.

dog ____   cat ____   spoon ____   fork ____   boy ____   girl ____   desk ____   book ____

6 Some plurals end in 's'. Some end in 'es'. Add 's' or 'es' to make each word into a plural.

shirt and dress   _____ and _____

bush and flower   _____ and _____

bag and box   _____ and _____

Little Red Riding Hood Story

Once upon a time, there was a little girl who lived in the woods with her mum. The girl's name was Little Red Riding Hood. One day, her mum called her to the kitchen.

"Please take this basket of food to Grandma," said Mum. "Be careful in the woods. Go straight to Grandma's house."

"I will, don't worry, Mum," called out Little Red Riding Hood as she skipped happily away with the basket.

Soon, she saw their friend the kind woodcutter. He was putting logs onto his truck and he waved to Little Red Riding Hood. She waved too and walked on through the woods.

Then, the big bad wolf stepped out from behind a tree.

"Little girl, where are you going?" he said, in a friendly voice.

"I'm going to see my grandma. I am going to be late!" said Little Red Riding Hood. She remembered what her mum had said about being careful and she ran away quickly. She looked back as she went but she could not see the wolf.

It was a long way to Grandma's house and she was tired when she got to the door.

"Grandma, I'm here!" called out Little Red Riding Hood.

Little Red Riding Hood Story

A voice said, "Come in, Little Red Riding Hood." So she went into the house. It was dark inside, but she could see someone sitting up in bed. Little Red Riding Hood thought Grandma looked funny.

"Grandma, what big eyes you have!" said Little Red Riding Hood.

"All the better for seeing you," said the voice.

"Grandma, what big ears you have!" said Little Red Riding Hood.

"All the better for hearing you," said the voice.

"Grandma, what big teeth you have!" said Little Red Riding Hood.

"All the better for gobbling you up!" said the voice. Little Red Riding Hood saw it was not Grandma. It was the big, bad wolf!

Just at that moment, in walked the woodcutter and scared the wolf away. "Never come back!" shouted the woodcutter. And the wolf never did.

Little Red Riding Hood heard someone say "Please, let me out!" She searched until she found Grandma shut in the cupboard. Grandma smiled. And they all lived happily ever after.